Think You Can and You Will

How to Become a Champion in Life

J. Steele

RWG Publishing
PO Box 596
Litchfield, IL 62056
https://rwgpublishing.com/

Published in the United States of America

CONTENTS

Introduction v

Chapter 1: Understanding the Game 1

Chapter 2: Devising a Plan 5

Thank You... 9

Introduction

How does one become a champion in life? What needs to happen before you can feel like you've won the game of life? The answer changes a lot from one person to the next as for some, it may mean to have a lot of money, and for others, it's about having great relationships, and for some, it's just about having a good time but what every one of these people have in common is that they have a hunger for a better life, they feel like their life can be something much more than what it currently is, you may be reading this book for that very same reason.

Whenever you ask people why they haven't been able to achieve whatever they are after yet, they always come up with the same answers. I didn't have enough time, money, resources, people, connections, backing, funding, investors, managers, employees, supervision, leadership, and the list can go on to infinity.

But what all of these things have in common is that they are resources, but the secret to being a champion in life is not having all the resources, but being resourceful is enough for anyone to get the result with the ones you do have while moving and hustling to get the ones you don't.

You know your life can be much greater than what you're currently experiencing, and while that is true, it is also true that you may be squandering what you already have in your life, not because there is something particularly wrong with you, but because we all tend to do this. We tend to take things we have for granted and daydream about what's missing in our lives, but in this particular book, you will learn the tools you need to override that natural brain programing and use new programs to have the kind of life you can be proud to share with others.

I will always remember what a friend of mine once told me during a challenging time in my life, I had just gotten fired from my job, and I was working two jobs that I hated just to make ends meet. So, I came complainingly to him talking about how bad I had it and how horrible my jobs were. I've always found it fascinating how, as human beings, we tend to compete with one another to see who has the worst life by saying things like, "oh, that's nothing! You should hear what happened to me…" always comparing scars like it should be something to be proud of, but I digress.

My friend patiently waited until I was done venting to him as I sat on his couch complaining about how much I hated my new jobs and how exhausted I was ending my sob story with the ultimate "I need a vacation."

My friend just looked up at me, he put his hands together and leaned in towards me to say:

"Instead of planning your next vacation, why not a life you don't need a break from?"

J. Steele

Chapter 1:

Understanding the Game

For you to win at any game or sports, you must understand the rules and how, and what series of actions will make you win, and if you don't understand the rules, it may be tough for you ever to be focused as you just don't know what's going on.
Have you ever played a game you didn't know or understood? Most likely, you had your butt handed to you before you even knew what was going on, right?

This is how exactly most people approach life, wanting so bad to win but having no clue as to how to do it, or how the rules work.

If you want to win in the game of life, you need to understand the rules, and believe it or not; the one writing the rules is not your boss, the economy, the president of the United Nations. You are the one writing the rules.

I'm not a child. I do realize there are things like laws and regulations, but laws and regulations won't make you happy, you will. And therefore, the real set of rules you need to follow to win at the game of life are your own.

First of all, you need to understand what rules you've already put in place, because believe it or not, the rules have already been written even though you may not be aware of it.

Figuring out the rules:

A dear friend of mine once told me this beautiful story about how he was trying to teach this very same concept to his ten-year-old daughter:

His daughter seamed anxious and angry, so he asked what was wrong. To this, his daughter replied that she couldn't organize her desk, no matter how many times she cleaned and organized it, it still seamed in her words "messy."

He asked her to take him to her desk, and she did; when they got there, the desk looked perfectly fine to him, but the little girl still saw a mess, so he just asked her, what exactly it messy? She said, "I don't know…"

He took one pencil and placed it in the middle of the desk, and he could see her face change, then he took an eraser and placed it next to the pencil when she screamed, "Dad! You're making a mess!" to which he responded, "if moving one pencil and an eraser is a mess to you, this desk will never be organized. It's not the desk that's messy, and it's your idea of what messy means…"

This applies to every area of our lives, as many times we want to be happy and fulfilled, but we have some particular rules about how we should obtain that, sometimes placed by ourselves and sometimes, imposed on us by others.

For you to figure out what your rules are, I want you to stop and do an exercise here with me:

Take a pen and paper, and I want you to write down the things you want in your life no matter how far fetched they may seem.

A car, a house, a happy marriage, a great relationship with your kids, a business, more time, more money, anything, and everything that you want to gain in your life.

Next to each item, I want you to write down how all of those things make you feel like a first gut reaction. Why? Because for example, some people may write down "more money," but when they read it, they may feel stressed like more money equals "more problems."

If one of your rules is more money = more problems, then until you change that rule, you will never be able to make more money as you're sending mixed signals to your brain, and for you to win at the game of life, you and your brain need to be on the same page at all times.

Analyze all of the items in your list and make sure you understand the rules you have for attaining these things, and then change the one that doesn't favor you, the cool thing about you writing the rules is that you can change whatever doesn't work for you.

Chapter 2:
Devising a Plan

Now that you understand the rules of the game, it's time to start developing a winning strategy, as the secret to winning in the game of life is to not just think about the things you want but to move towards them and take constant action to make them happen.

First things first.

You need a destination as your definite goal; for you to win, you need to understand what it is that will make you win.

Figure out what is the one thing that you would give everything and go to any length to attain. For some, it's being able to travel around the world, and for others, it's owning a fortune 500 company. Though the goals are different, but the method is the same.

Figure out what your goal is – your destination. And after that, you need to devise a plan of how you're going to get there, work your way backward from your goal to the actions and resources you need to get there.

I want you to take out another piece of paper, and on this one, I want you to write down your goal at the top. After that, I want you to write down all the resources you need to make it happen – that means time, money, connections, people, knowledge, information, etc.

Next, write down all the actions you need to take to achieve this goal – Who do you need to talk to? What do you need to write? Do you need to train? What do you need to learn? – once you have this on paper, you will have some idea of how you can attain this goal you want so badly.

And make no mistake, you need to want it badly, if your goal doesn't keep you awake at night and makes you jump out of bed in excitement, then your goal is not your true goal. Some people lie to themselves by saying they want a million dollars, but in reality, they just want to help others and travel around the world, the actions are more exciting than the money.

Don't just sit there and tell yourself that you want a million dollars. You should ask yourself what a million dollars will get you that you don't already have, that's your true goal?

Training For The Gold:

Whenever you see a top athlete try to claim a championship, you see them train for months, or even years before the event. They don't just show up and compete, but they take actions every single day that get them closer and closer to their goal, one bite-sized action at a time.

Most people attempt to attain their goal in one try, and if they fail, they give up. What most successful people have figured out is that it takes a lot of actions and a lot of failures and corrections to get it right, much like an athlete preparing to compete for the gold.

One thing you must know upfront is that you will without a single doubt make mistakes, and you will fail at some point, and I'm not saying this to discourage you or put you down, but I'm saying this because it's a fact of life you need to be ready for. So, if you're expecting to be perfect and everything to go your way, you will end up throwing everything away due to the frustration of not meeting your expectations. But if you understand this is part of the process, you will not get discouraged, and you will simply learn from what went wrong, make adjustments, and keep moving forward.

This is what you should do every time you find yourself facing challenges or setbacks regardless of how big they might be, if your goal is worth it, you will push through anything and find a way to get it done. Also, remember that it's the small daily actions that translate into huge results.

As a final and vital exercise, I want you to grab a notebook, and this is going to be somewhat of a diary for you, I want you to write on it every single day, and this is what you're going to write on it:

-        Your Goals for the Month:

The goals you want to accomplish that month, all the things you know you need to have accomplished that month to get closer to your goal.

-        What You are Grateful For:

Write down all the things you're grateful for that day. This will not only help you have a clear perspective on your emotions but also your resources. It helps you understand where you stand without the feeling of overwhelm.

-        Your To-Do List:

Write down all the things you need to do that day and always include, at least, one or more things that are related to your goal. This helps you have a clear picture of how much action you're taking towards reaching your goals.

Thank You

9

That's all for now, I hope you've enjoyed this book, and I hope it is useful for you in your life, I wish you nothing but the greatest of successes, and I want to thank you for getting to the end, you are now one step closer to becoming a true champion in life.

Thank you

J. Steele